Saving Your Life
*Way of*

# The Silver Solution

By L.J. Silver
Copyright 2014

## Dedication

This book is dedicated to Americans of modest means; Americans to whom achieving the Great American Dream may seem impossible since the financial crisis of 2008.

## Table of Contents

| | |
|---|---|
| 1 | Preface |
| 2 | Why Write This Book |
| 3 | The Problem |
| 4 | The Case for Gold |
| 5 | The Better Case for Silver |
| 6 | Classes of Silver Assets |
| 7 | A Simple Plan |
| 8 | What to Buy |
| 9 | Where to Buy |
| 10 | Safe Storage |

# 1      Preface

*"If we are wise, let us prepare for the worst."*

-George Washington

Most economists foresee the financial disaster that awaits the United States. They know that the massive money printing experiment that began in 2008 will not end well. But most aren't talking; at least not publicly.

They can't. Most economists work for the government, or "Wall Street," or huge multinational corporations. And it is not in these organizations' best interest for the public to know what is coming.

Economists employed by investment banks and huge corporations do not have a public forum, and their employers do not want the public to know what is coming. It would be bad for business.

The well-informed, the powerful, and the rich are taking steps to preserve their way of life during the economic tsunami that they know is just over the horizon.

Wall Street, the Federal Reserve and the other central banks around the world see what's coming, but dare not hint at the insurmountable problems lest they cause panic on Main Street. Main Street is us. It refers to us so-called 99 per centers.

What can Americans of modest means do to preserve their way of life? It's relatively simple. I started about five years ago. If your assets, modest as they may be, are not protected from what awaits America, start now. The beginning of the end will probably start in the U.S. sometime between 2016 and 2019. You still have time.

The data, facts, and figures presented in this book are available from many reliable sources, including the Congressional Budget Office, www.whitehouse.org, and the Saint Louis Reserve Bank, to name just a few. I do not footnote or often list references because the information is so widely available.

Note: I have used a pen name. While I don't think the coming economic collapse will result in bands of roaming thieves; thieves who may think the author of *The Silver Solution* and his relatives and associates have hoards of silver in their houses, one cannot be too careful.

# 2    Why Write This Book

Even though you have little by way of assets, and your income modest, you can prepare for, and even improve your economic circumstances during the turmoil of the next several years. This book is meant to be the encouragement and the "how-to" to do just that. You can survive economically, and maybe even prosper.

I am a middle aged, middle class, husband, father, and grandfather who doesn't have enough savings to see me through retirement in the difficult economic times we face in the two to three decades ahead-- much less have something left to pass on to those children and grandchildren. I am fast approaching retirement age, but cannot afford to retire. A growing number of baby boomers are in this same situation.

In 2007 most of my modest net worth was tied up in three real estate properties, one of which was my home in northern California. The other two properties were investment properties in other states. In 2007, I thought the value of that real estate would continue to grow as it had my whole life and that I would be in good financial shape for retirement in a few years.

The value of land never goes down, right? After all "… they aren't making any more of it." By the end of 2008 my real estate was worth less than I owed the banks. My self-directed IRA took a big hit when the markets crashed. My net worth was suddenly about zero. And I already knew social security would not be enough to live on in retirement.

In 2009 I learned what caused the real estate and stock market crash in 2008, and why. More importantly, I learned that the financial crisis that occurred in 2008 was just the first act. Two more acts will play out over the next several years. The worst, by far, is yet to come.

I began looking for another way, besides real estate appreciation and investing in the stock market, to get into a position to retire in a few years. Through my research, I realized that my real estate would never again be worth what it was at the peak in 2007, after allowing for inflation. I also had to admit that I'm not very good at investing in the stock market.

My formal education includes a Bachelor of Science in Business Administration and a Masters degree in Business Administration; both from highly ranked universities. For over thirty years, I have worked as a Manager in manufacturing companies; multi-billion dollar corporations, medium sized corporations, and tiny startup companies.

With all of that going for me; plus the fact that I was born a citizen of the United States of America, I should have been able to achieve The Great American Dream and retire in comfort at an early age. But the financial crisis of 2008, which occurred when I was in my mid-fifties, was a serious setback. And the next big leg down in the economy will be much worse than the jolt suffered in 2008.

Knowledge is power. Had I known the financial crisis of 2008 was coming in 2006, I could have taken steps to preserve my modest wealth, and may have even increased it. Having learned what caused the financial crisis in 2008 and what the next stage of economic collapse will look like, I now stay abreast of developments and work my plan to protect and grow my assets during the troubling times ahead.

I read multiple articles a day about the economy six days a week; not just the U.S. economy, but European and Asian economies too. After all, it's a global economy. What happens in one economy affects the economy of other countries...eventually.

I also read a couple of new books on macro economics each year and subscribe to semi-monthly macroeconomic reports published by the leading independent macroeconomists in the U.S.; macro-economists who work for themselves and are free to publish their research and opinions without the censorship of their employer or the government.

I emphatically <u>do not</u> pay attention to economic news published by the so-called main stream media, which is all carefully edited to keep us sheep in line to be systematically sheared—economically speaking.

I know economics and financial planning is boring to most people. But I love it. And traditional financial planners have a vested interest in keeping us doing the same thing we have always done.

In this book, the sum total of over five years of research and continuous monitoring of macroeconomic conditions is distilled into a simple plan to help the typical American of modest means avoid, or at least minimize, the devastating effect of the economic tsunami that could hit the U.S. at any time. It is the plan I began to use in 2009.

Thankfully, my circumstances have improved since I implemented this plan, and my income is now beyond modest. But I am still following the same general plan.

I have three grown children who have families of their own. They are "men of modest means." Economic conditions are much more difficult for my children's generation than they were for me. Even the so-called good jobs do not pay as much as they did thirty years ago, relative to the current cost of living. And they are going to face this economic tsunami mid-career, with children in school.

As mentioned above, phase 2 of the economic difficulties the U.S. faces will probably not hit before 2016. And it might not hit until around 2019. But it will hit. And when it does, the value of all traditional financial assets; stocks, bonds, and real estate, will be devastated by a huge multi-year wave of inflation.

*An economic tsunami will decimate traditional assets*

Americans must do something different to merely keep their asset value static in the face of this tsunami of inflation, much less increase it.

# 3     The Problem

Virtually all developed and developing economies in the world have been living on borrowed money for decades. Norway and Switzerland are still in pretty good shape. But their economies are small. Germany is in pretty good shape, and is the fourth largest economy in the world, but Germany is part of the troubled Eurozone. The weaker Eurozone economies like Greece, Spain, Italy, and France will drag Germany down. Or to put it another way, Germany cannot save all of these other countries in the Eurozone. And neither can the U.S. The U.S. can't even save itself from this disaster of its own making. And all the other countries in the world combined, even if they wanted to, cannot save the U.S.

Since 2007, deficit spending by the federal government has more-or-less tripled in the U.S. Many countries have gone past the point of no return with their national public debt. By that I mean there is no way they can ever repay the national debt. The only hope is to inflate their currency so they can repay in cheaper "dollars" (or yen, or lire, or euros, or marks, etc). As of this writing, the U.S. public debt is approaching $18 trillion. That is $18,000,000,000,000.

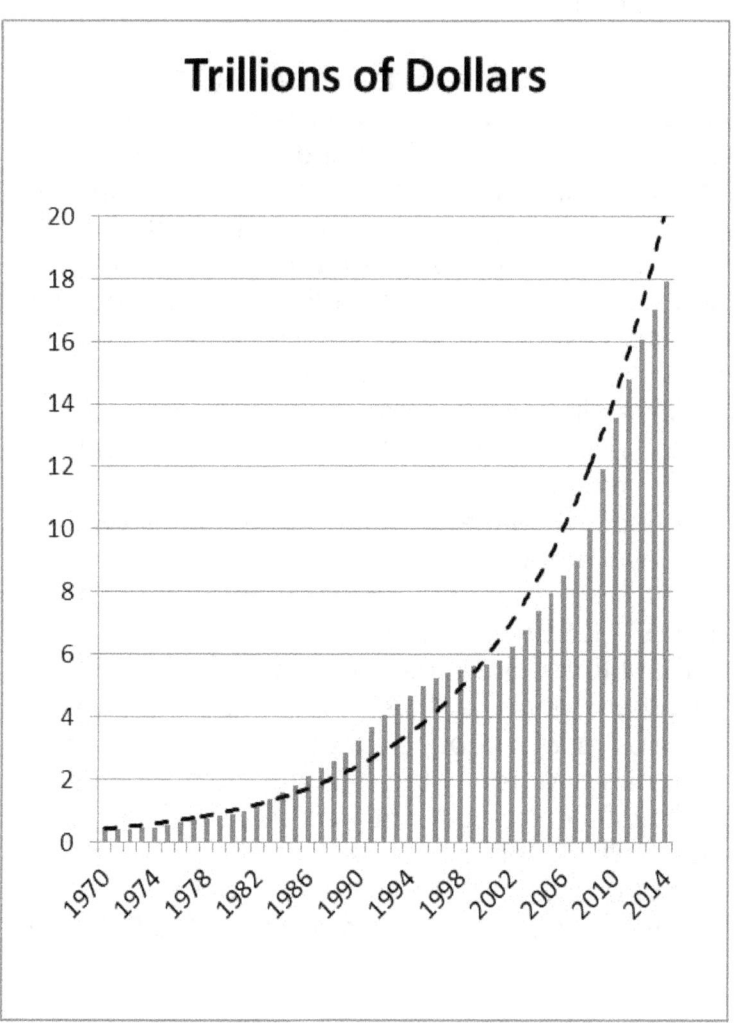

*The U.S. government will never be able to repay its debt.*

And this number does not include unfunded liabilities such as Social Security and government pensions. Estimates of unfunded federal government liabilities range between $120 trillion and $200 trillion. On average in recent years, the U.S. federal government takes in about $2.5 trillion a year and spends about $3.5 trillion a year. It must borrow an extra $1 trillion each year.

The public debt is so high in the U.S. that the government can no longer borrow all it needs at interest rates that it can afford to pay. There is too little investment money available in the world to buy all the new U.S. debt being issued each year. The U.S. government can attract more of the investment money that is available in the world by paying higher rates. But higher interest payments just make the amount the U.S. needs to borrow increase even more, pushing the debt level higher. It is a vicious cycle.

The short-term solution is to print more money and to use this money to buy the debt that investors will not or cannot buy. The Federal Reserve has been buying an increasing percentage of U.S. treasuries since 2009, and doing so with dollars created with keystrokes on a computer (referred to as "printing money). The more of something there is, the less it is worth. When it comes to money, this decrease in value is called inflation.

And this is the crux of the matter for you and me.

Inflated dollars will buy less in the future—much less. Our incomes will not rise at nearly the same rate as our cost of living does. And those on a fixed income will suffer the most. Although Social Security and many government pensions are tied to a cost of living index, these indexes are rigged so that recipients do not receive increases anywhere near the real increase in their cost of living.

The government and many economists point to their rigged inflation indexes and tell us that inflation in the U.S. is running about 1.5% per year. The real rate of inflation in 2013 was probably between 6% and 8%, and will likely stay in that range for two to five years more. When inflation begins in earnest, the Federal Reserve and government will not be able to control it.

You may have heard of the hyper inflation that beset post-WWI Germany, the Weimar Republic. It got so bad that it took a wheel barrow load of German marks to buy a loaf of bread...then it got worse. The price of everything rose daily, and then hourly.

Those who could afford to eat out were given a cost estimate when they ordered their meal, but the final price for the meal was based on replacement cost of the dish eaten at the time their bill was presented. Those who ate slowly paid more. Chewing each bite twenty-two times might have been good advice for digestion, but it wasn't good economic advice.

The Weimar Republic is probably the best-known case of hyper-inflation. Hyper-inflation is generally agreed by economists to be a rate of inflation that reaches 50% or more <u>per month</u>.

To demonstrate how devastating hyper-inflation is, if inflation is 50% per month for twelve months in a row, the total inflation for one year would be 12,975%. That is; goods will cost almost 130 times more after one year. Or to put it another way, it would take $130 to buy what $1 bought just twelve months earlier.

The Weimar Republic printed money to pay off its war debts; lots of money. The more it printed, the more the German mark devalued. Devaluation of a currency is inflation. The more the mark decreased in value, the more marks the Weimer Republic had to print. Hyper-inflation ensued and the currency literally wasn't worth the paper used to print it.

Since the Weimar Republic, there have been twenty-seven cases of hyper-inflation around the world. In twenty-seven out of twenty-seven cases, hyper-inflation was caused by the respective government printing large amounts of its currency to pay off government debt, just like the Weimar Republic did. Just like the U.S. began doing in 2009.

In the first paragraph of this chapter I stated that "virtually all developed and developing economies in the world have been living on of borrowed money for decades." Almost all of these countries have hit a wall; they can no longer borrow enough to cover current spending plus the amount necessary to pay off the borrowing done in previous years.

So what are they doing? They are creating large amounts of currency and buying their own debt; just like the U.S. is doing. Countries no longer create money by printing it. They create money with a few keystrokes on a computer.

In the U.S., the Federal Reserve is lending newly created dollars to the government through the mechanism of buying government bonds. The U.S. Federal Reserve began buying some of U.S. debt in 2009. Why? Because there weren't enough buyers of U.S. treasuries to buy the approximately additional $1 trillion every year to fund the Federal government's annual deficit spending.

It is estimated that the Federal Reserve bought 61% of U.S. debt in 2011, 70% in 2012, and about 80% in 2013. It was all done with dollars created out of thin air by the Federal Reserve, the central bank of the U.S., which is responsible for protecting the value of the U.S. dollar.

By the way, in the 100 years since the Federal Reserve was established in 1913, the dollar has lost 99% of its buying power.

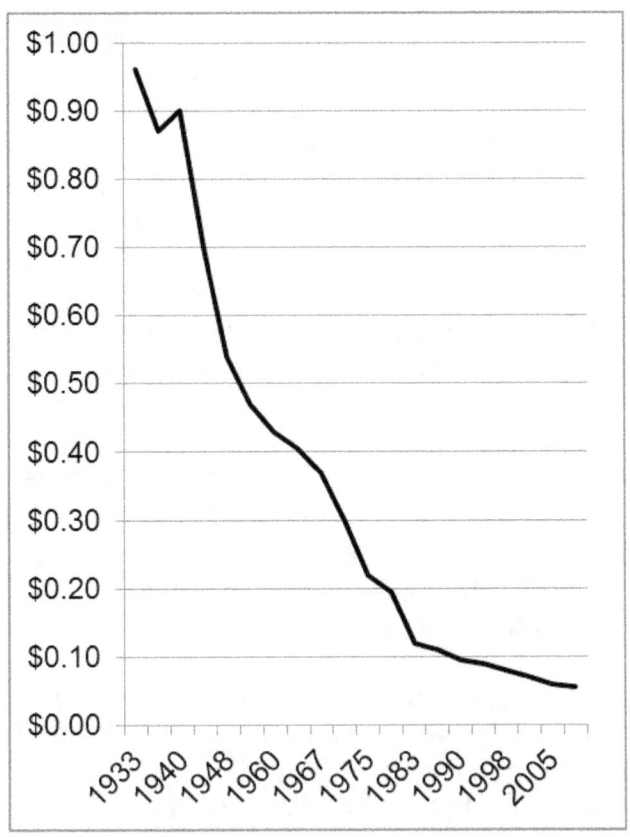

**Loss in Value of U.S. Dollar 1933 - 2008**

The money supply in the US increased from 800 billion dollars in 2007 to 4 trillion dollars (4,000 billion) at the end of 2013.  That is a 400% increase in six years.  Did the economy grow 400%, and therefore require the extra dollars in circulation to grease the wheels of commerce? Of course not, the U.S. economy is struggling to grow 2% a year. What grew was government spending. Total deficit spending for 2008 through 2013 alone was $5.726 trillion, an average of .9573 trillion dollars per year. (www.whitehouse.gov/omb/budget/Historicals)

Most economists, and, in my opinion, all central bankers, such as the Federal Reserve in the U.S., know where this unprecedented level of money creation will lead. It will lead to INFLATION—which is the devaluation of currency, or the loss of buying power.

I didn't I write "all economists" in the paragraph above because not everyone with a PhD agrees that two plus two equals four. Some think two plus two equals five, or six, or eight; especially, it seems, those currently advising the U.S. government.

Despite a hundred years of history to the contrary, a few think it will be different this time. They think that high inflation cannot happen in the U.S. They think the U.S. is special, or that our central bankers are smarter than those of other countries. And for the most part, these are the economists whose ideas get published by the main stream media and quoted by our politicians.

How else can we sheep be kept in line to be sheared?

I'm stepping out of the sheep-shearing line. In the U.S. we still have the freedom to get out of the line. We have the freedom to think for ourselves, though an increasing number of Americans choose not to do so. Most Americans stay in line voluntarily. They stay in the line because of misinformation; misinformation that tells them that the financial crisis of 2008 was a fluke and if they just keep doing what they have always done they can still achieve The Great American Dream.

When a small percentage of the public see the economic tsunami coming and take action to protect their assets, say 20%, the government's game is over. The fragile economy will deteriorate quickly right past economic recession and into economic depression. By then, a vast number of "sheep" will have already been shorn. They will have no wool (assets) left to protect them from the cold economic reality that will be the new norm. They will be dependent on the generosity of the U.S. government. But the U.S. government is already broke—beyond broke. In those times the U.S. government will not be able to borrow at all, and additional money creation will result in even higher inflation. Higher inflation means our dollars will buy even less.

The "U.S." is not smarter than everyone else in the world. It will not defy the economic laws of supply and demand that have governed since people used sea shells for money. If the U.S. is smarter, it wouldn't be taking the same economic path that put so many European countries in such weak financial positions today. It wouldn't be taking the same path that resulted in hyperinflation for 27 countries in the past 100 years.

And there will be no one to help the U.S. First, the U.S. economy is so big and the economic problems so huge that all the other industrialized nations combined are not enough. Second, many countries are jealous of the economic success of the U.S. and wouldn't help even if they could. They want to see the U.S. fail. They want the U.S. to get its comeuppance. And it will. Economic laws apply to the U.S. too, just as physical laws, such as gravity, apply equally around the world.

Unfortunately, the middle class in the U.S. will suffer most. The vast middle class will suffer most because that is where most of the asset value is held in the U.S. The few super rich, the "one per centers," just do not have enough to make a difference.

Inflation in Venezuela is 60% per year (fall of 2014). In Argentina inflation is now running about 26% per year. When the official inflation rate hits 8% to 10% in the U.S., many people will wake up to the reality that this time is different.

It will not take hyper-inflation to devastate the U.S. economy and asset values. And the Federal Reserve and other central banks around the world know it. Only moderately high inflation for several years, like the U.S. experienced in the late 1970s and early 1980s, will be devastating.

In early 2014, president Obama proposed a federal budget of $3.9 trillion, the highest in the history of the country. Money creation must continue to support this extreme level of spending. And money creation causes inflation.

In 2009 the U.S. treasury could no longer sell enough treasuries (borrow) to fund all of its annual spending. That's when the money creation started in earnest in the U.S. Anyone in Congress or in the mainstream media who dares admit that all this money creation is a problem is scoffed at and vilified. Government officials say massive money creation is not a problem and publish ten-year projections to prove that everything is under control.

Ten year government projections are never correct. Not even the first year is correct, much less the next nine. If an honest ten-year projection was published, many people would stop spending and start saving. And the economy would go into a tailspin.

Look at it this way, if creating money to run the government isn't a bad thing to do, why not create all the money the government wants? Why not eliminate federal income tax and create the full $3.9 trillion a year instead of only the approximately $1 trillion a year annual deficit?

In the U.S., the Federal Reserve controls money creation. The Federal Reserve knows that extreme levels of money creation will eventually result in inflation. Central banks around the world know it, investment banks know it, commercial banks know it, and large corporations know it. They are all preparing for inflation. They are positioning to not only survive, but to profit from U.S. inflation at the expense of the middle class in the U.S., because that is where the vast wealth of the U.S. is held.

That's why the banks in the U.S. are sitting on almost $2 trillion dollars instead of lending it out to businesses and individuals. They know their loans would be repaid in inflated dollars, dollars worth much less than the dollars they lend. They also know the loans are risky because of the shaky U.S. economy.

The only way to avoid inflation is for the Federal Reserve to pull the excess money back; that is, take it out of circulation; destroy it. But to pull those created dollars back, the federal government must spend less than it takes in. And that's politically impossible.

To merely avoid creating more dollars, the federal government must balance its budget–NOW. And we all know that will not happen. Politicians who vote to reduce spending will be voted out of office.

To reduce the money supply, the government must reduce its spending to an amount less than it collects. If average borrowing, and therefore money creation, is a trillion dollars a year, the government must spend a trillion dollars less to just halt the money creation. That means the proposed $3.9 trillion budget must be cut to $2.9 trillion. That is a reduction of over 25%. Reduced spending is called austerity.

A couple of European countries have tried austerity recently, and it was not received well by the public. There was rioting in the streets and the politicians who tried it were voted out of power.

In France in 2012, the socialist party was voted into power. The socialist leader promised to cease austerity programs and to restore government welfare programs to previous levels. It didn't work of course. In April 2014 the socialist government is moving back toward capitalism and austerity, and is now in danger of being voted out of office.

In summary; in the ninety-five years since the Weimar Republic suffered through hyper inflation, there have been twenty-seven cases of hyper-inflation around the world. In all cases, hyper inflation was brought about by printing/creating massive amounts of the country's currency for the purpose of paying government debt.

I do not think the U.S. will encounter hyper-inflation, which is defined as 50% or more per month. But several years of moderate to high inflation will be devastating to the typical American. Consider the loss of buying power of the U.S. dollar if inflation gradually increased to 100% a year (about 7% per month) and stayed there just two years before falling back to modest levels:

| Year | Annual Inflation | $1 buying power | cum. % loss |
| --- | --- | --- | --- |
| 1 | 6% | .94 | 6% |
| 2 | 10% | .86 | 14% |
| 3 | 15% | .75 | 25% |
| 4 | 25% | .60 | 40% |
| 5 | 50% | .40 | 60% |
| 6 | 80% | .22 | 78% |
| 7 | 100% | .11 | 89% |
| 8 | 100% | .06 | 94% |
| 9 | 50% | .04 | 96% |
| 10 | 15% | .03 | 97% |

The cumulative loss of buying power of the U.S. dollar would be 97% if the U.S. experiences ten years of inflation as depicted above. It will take $100 to buy what $3 bought just ten years earlier.

Will wages rise? Sure. But they will not rise anywhere near as fast as inflation destroys buying power. This is the primary way the working men and women of America will be sheared if they do not break away from the heard.

Inflation is the devaluation of a currency. This devaluation results from the creation of much more money than is required to support the level of economic growth of the country. If you believe the official numbers, and I do not, the U.S. economy has been growing at about 2% per year. Over a recent six-year period that the money supply was increased 400% the economy grew less than 12%.

Inflation will hit the U.S. When it does, the combined net worth of the huge middle class in the U.S. will be destroyed. The value of stocks, bonds, and real estate will plummet.

I've not attempted to show the casual effects between inflation and the devastation it will cause to the value of real estate, stocks, and bonds. Others do so much better than I can. I have nothing original to contribute to that discussion. But you need to know the root cause. The root cause is money creation. Money creation leads to inflation. It always has, and always will.

*"Inflation is always and everywhere a monetary phenomenon."*
-Milton Friedman, recipient of the 1976 Nobel Memorial Prize in Economic Sciences

If you are interested in learning what happened in 2008 and what is yet to come, I recommend "*Aftershock*" by Wiedemer, Wiedemer, and Spitzer

I hope this chapter scares you; scares you into action. Modest steps taken now can make a huge difference to your financial security a few years from now. You can have more financial security during the difficult times ahead than you have now during the not-so-bad times.

# 4    The Case for Gold

I read a great deal about gold. Few credible gold analysts have been right about gold in the last three to four years.

And I am wary of predictions and analysis provided by the investment banks. I believe that investment banks, or some of them, perhaps acting at the behest of the Federal Reserve at times, have manipulated the price of gold downward since 2011.

Why would the Federal Reserve care about the price of gold? Because gold is priced in U.S. dollars the world over, and as the price of gold rises, investment capital will move out of U.S. treasuries and other dollar–denominated investments and into gold. To attract investment capital to U.S. treasuries when the price of gold is rising, yields (commonly referred to as interest) must rise. Rising yields cost the U.S. government more to borrow to fund the annual deficit.

When interest rates rise, the cost of borrowing goes up. When the cost of borrowing goes up, the government must borrow even more to pay the higher interest costs, and the Federal Reserve must create even more dollars. Creating more dollars causes more inflation, which pushes interest rates up even more. Once this cycle takes over, a country cannot stop it without causing an immediate and total collapse of its economy.

In mid 2014 I estimate that articles written by gold analysts are about 50% bullish and 50% bearish. In the next year or so, at least half of these experts will be right; the price of gold will rise (bullish prediction), or it will fall (bearish prediction). I wouldn't be surprised if the price of gold rose and fell, or fell and rose, and then all the experts will claim another accurate prediction on gold.

Most of the bears seem to be technicians; that is, they read and interpret the historical price charts. Some bulls are technicians. They read those same charts and somehow arrive at the opposite conclusion. However, most of the bulls that have an established track record with gold cite the fundamentals for their bullish position on gold.

However, if manipulation of the price of gold in the futures markets is going on, and I firmly believe it is, then the charts aren't very useful. Only the manipulators know when more manipulation will take place. Charts cannot predict manipulation. And in my opinion, price manipulation is more likely to take place when the charts are bullish, because that is the time that downward price manipulation will cause the most financial pain to the gold investors and speculators who placed bets on a price increase.

What do I mean by manipulation? I mean that on several occasions, large quantities of gold have been sold all at once, forcing the price to move down sharply. Not only were the sell quantities unusually large, the sale was often done on the lightly-traded

24-hour gold market at night when the major markets were closed.

The largest gold market is the London gold exchange. The second largest is the New York gold exchange. At two AM New York time, neither market is open. When a 100 million or 200 million ounces hits the market in the wee hours of the morning New York time, there are not enough buyers to absorb the supply. Price drops sharply. Gold investors suffer heavy losses while they sleep. Gold investors become wary of again investing in gold.

I define these huge gold sales as manipulation because a gold investor cannot make money selling gold in this manner. The rational manner in which to sell a large quantity of gold is to sell it a little at a time over several days or weeks when the London or New York gold exchanges are open and there are many buyers.

My purpose here is to provide the big picture, the world macroeconomic view. Gold will provide great asset protection in every country that experiences high inflation. Over several years, the U.S. dollar will probably experience the highest inflation of any major currency, because the surplus money already created and yet to be created surpasses that of any other country.

Gold is one of the few assets available to us commoners to protect our assets in the coming economic tsunami. What follows is some of the fundamental data regarding gold.

- Ninety to ninety-five percent of all the gold ever mined is still in existence today.
- At $1,600 per troy ounce, all this gold has a value of about $9 trillion.
- If all the gold every mined was melted and cast into a cube, that cube would be about 70 feet per side.
- All the gold ever mined would fill about 3.5 Olympic sized swimming pools.
- According to the U.S. Treasury records, the U.S. Treasury possesses about $350 billion in gold. (a little more than 1/3 of a trillion dollars)

Gold is a global commodity, and is priced in U.S. dollars. The value of all assets in the U.S. at the end of 2013, according to the Federal Reserve, is $177 trillion (primarily, stocks + bonds + real estate). In 2012, a global management consulting company estimated that total world asset value was $600 trillion.

Value of world gold supply = $9 trillion
Value of all U.S. assets = $177 trillion
Value of global assets = $600 trillion

By doing some arithmetic, you can determine that the value of all gold is 5% of the value of all assets in the U.S. It is only 1.5% of the value of global assets. When these other assets begin losing value due to inflation (caused by massive money creation around the globe), a portion of these assets will be converted into gold.

Why? Because gold has been the preferred means to store value in troubled economic times for centuries.

From 1971, when President Nixon took the U.S. off of the gold standard, until 1980, the price of gold rose from an artificial low of $35 per ounce to $800 per ounce. During the late 1970s and early 1980s, annual inflation in the U.S. reached a high of about 15% per year.

Cumulative inflation in the U.S. during this period of time was about 100%. But the price of gold rose 2,200%.

Granted, the official price of gold in the U.S. was artificially low in 1971. But even if the free-market price was double the official price of $35, there was still a 1,100% increase in the price of gold for those holding U.S. dollars.

Why did the price of gold rise 2,200% when inflation was only 100%? The outsized increase in the price of gold resulted from the FEAR of inflation by a small percentage of U.S. citizens. An even smaller percentage feared hyper inflation and total economic collapse and bid the price of gold up to $800 per ounce.

Incidentally, allowing for inflation in the U.S. since 1980, an $800 per ounce price of gold in 1980 is equivalent to about a $2,200 per ounce price in 2014.

Few people in the U.S. fear inflation in 2014. Some economists say deflation is the danger, not inflation.

In the past few years, about 20% of all gold produced has been bought by Indians, as in, citizens of India, not Native Americans. In 2013 China surpassed India as the biggest buyer of gold. China is now buying over 20% of all the gold produced each year. Despite being the richest nation in the world, the U.S. has only been buying about 10% of global production.

If we assume that U.S. citizens and companies own 10% of all the gold there is, that means we own only about $900 billion dollars worth of gold ($9 trillion value of world supply x 10%).

When inflation becomes an issue in the U.S., the $177 trillion of dollars in assets owned by U.S. citizens will be looking to a mere $9 trillion world-wide gold supply for safety and insurance against inflation.

These U.S. citizens will be competing with people in the rest of the world for a share of that $9 trillion in gold. If inflation hits elsewhere before it hits the U.S., citizens of other nations will start moving assets into gold before the uninformed citizens of the U.S. begin moving their assets into gold.

I wrote "uniformed" above. Perhaps I should have written "misinformed." The main-stream media in the U.S. is overwhelmingly liberal, and publishes all the positive news and puts a positive spin on it while virtually ignoring the negative economic news. They do this to mask the absolute failure of the current administration's economic policies. I am not blaming the current administration for the problems the U.S. faces. The problem has been building to this for decades. I am merely pointing out the reason that the media does not give criticism where criticism is due at this time. We sheeple must be kept in line. The liberal media act as sheeple herders.

Stock brokers, banks, the Federal Reserve, and the U.S. government also benefit by keeping the masses misinformed. They want both our money and foreign investor money invested in U.S. real estate, stocks, and bonds. That is how they make money. Banks do not make money when we buy gold. And the purchase of gold does not help the struggling U.S. economy.

The informed people who have money are quietly buying gold. For three years now, the Chinese central government has been encouraging Chinese citizens to buy gold and silver. In Singapore, one can buy gold at an ATM at the mall.

One other aspect I will touch on is Germany's gold held by the U.S. Treasury. Germany moved 15% of its gold reserves to the U.S. for safe keeping after WW II.

The Federal Reserve claims to have much more gold than any other central bank in the world. However, when Germany asked for the return of its gold, the Federal Reserve "stuttered around" for awhile before it finally said it would need seven years to comply.

The amount of gold that Germany requested is a tiny percentage of the gold that the U.S. Treasury claims to hold. Also, in late 2013, the U.S. Treasury refused to allow a third-party audit of its gold holdings on behalf of Germany. Needless to say, speculation is rampant amongst the conspiracy theorists. Does the U.S. Treasury have as much gold as it claims to have?

If it doesn't, when that fact becomes known, faith in the U.S. dollar will crumble. Its value against other currencies will plummet. Investment money will flee the U.S. The price of gold will soar.

In late 2013 and early 2014 there were rumors of shortages of physical gold. In late 2012 in India, people were paying as much as $130 an ounce above the spot price of gold in the futures market for physical gold. That is; when the spot price of gold was $1,250 an ounce, Indians were paying as much as $1,380 per ounce to obtain physical gold.

When demand for physical gold spikes due to fear of inflation, people will buy all they can afford and manipulation of the price of gold will cease. That doesn't mean it will be smooth sailing for gold investors. And, just as it was in the late 1970s and early 1980s in the U.S., the price of gold will be very volatile.

If you do not read financial publications and rely only on the so-called main stream media, you haven't heard of the manipulation of the price of gold. Even business television steers clear of the subject.

In summary, when moderately higher levels of inflation hit the U.S., a small percentage of people will transfer some of their assets into gold. Another small percentage of people will fear that the moderate levels of inflation will fast become high levels, and they will buy more gold.

In my opinion, it will be the FEAR of inflation that will send the price of gold skyward. I believe that the run up in the price of gold will far exceed the actual inflation experienced in the U.S. (Remember; inflation is actually devaluation of the dollar). At some point in the years ahead, I believe the price of gold will hit outrageously high levels. Gold will eventually become the biggest asset bubble of all-time.

But this book is written for Americans of modest means.

If one only has $30 or even $200 a month to insure one's future against inflation, gold is not the way to go. Buying such a tiny amount of gold is outrageously expensive due to high transaction costs.

# 5    The Better Case for Silver

As good as the case for gold is, in my opinion, the case for silver is even better.

First, whereas over 90% of the gold ever mined is still available, over 90% of the silver ever mined is gone, and gone forever. Hundreds of millions of tons of silver are buried in landfills all over the world. A large portion of the recently mined silver exists in minute quantities in over 1,000 different products all over the world. It is impractical to recover these minute amounts of silver scattered all over the world.

The value of all the above-ground silver is approximately $30 billion at today's prices. $30 billion is less than ½ of 1% of the $9 trillion value of all the physical gold in the world. If a single multi-billionaire wanted to, he/she could buy $3 billion of physical silver and send the price of silver soaring.

After all, in 1980 when the Hunt brothers of Texas pushed the price of silver to $49 and change, they had only cornered about 8.5% of the market.

Second, industrial use of silver is much higher than that of gold. Less than 20% of the gold mined each year is used by industry, including electronics and dentistry. Silver, on the other hand, sees over 50% of annual production consumed by industry, largely electronics, with a growing percentage from solar panel production. Silver is the world's best conductor of electricity and heat, best natural biocide, and best reflector of light. Additional industrial applications for silver continue to be discovered every year.

Because of its excellent electrical conductive qualities, there is no substitute, especially in the world of miniature electronic applications. The cost of silver as a percentage of total fabrication cost is very low in most products, 2% or less for many.

At 2%, when the cost of silver increases fivefold, the percentage of total product cost resulting from silver increases to 10%. Manufacturers will pay any price for silver; there is no substitute. They must pay the price to continue to produce their products and stay in business. They will simply raise their price 10%--or more likely, 15%.

To summarize so far, silver inventory is low, but demand for industrial applications is high and rising. Now let's look at supply.

Third, there are only about two dozen silver mines in the world. That is, mines with the primary purpose of mining silver. Two dozen mines across the globe are not very many. And these two dozen mines only produce about 30% of the silver mined each year.

Most metal ore mines produce two or more metals. But there is always a primary metal, the reason the mine exists. The other metals are not present in sufficient quantity to make it cost effective, but since the ore is being processed anyway, refining and selling these other metals reduces the cost of mining the primary metal being mined.

About 70% of all the silver mined each year is mined as a by-product of other metals mining, such as copper, zinc, and nickel. This means silver production cannot be easily increased as demand for silver increases. And if mining operations of other industrial metals shut down or slow down due to economic recession or depression, the production of silver as a byproduct ceases or slows also.

But when world economies slow and the demand for silver drops, demand for silver will not slow as much as industrial products using copper, aluminum, and steel. The world runs on electronic gadgets. Even some of the homeless in the U.S. have cell phones.

<u>Fourth</u>, when the price of gold makes the first big move up, silver will become the "poor man's gold. By-and-large, Americans are not aware of the need for "asset protection" and the role gold plays in protecting assets from inflation.

When middle class Americans once again see the value of their 401k and real estate quickly drop by 40% to 50% as it did in 2008, many will look for other means to protect their dwindling assets against inflation. Gold has played that role around the world for centuries, and it will again.

If inflation hits other large economies first, and it may well do so, citizens of those countries will flock to gold and push the price up before U.S. citizens know they have a problem. By the time the more informed American middle class become aware, the price of gold will have shot up to new all-time highs. Half of the "gold experts" will be claiming that this is just the resumption of a huge bull run in gold, which I believe will be correct. The other half will claim that the price of gold is in bubble territory and is sure to plummet any day.

Many Americans will convert a portion of their dwindling assets to "poor man's gold," silver. No one can predict when this will happen and what the price of gold and silver will be at that time. But I can easily imagine a scenario in which the first wave of American middle class latecomers view $100 per ounce silver as a better buy than $3,000 per ounce gold.

In inflationary times, the wealthy of all nations have turned to gold, except the Germans. Germans have preferred silver in the past. I don't know why.

However, in the spirit of full disclosure, my ancestry puts me at about 98% German. Maybe my preference for silver is in my genes, not my analysis (just joking).

A couple of other observations: China is the largest producer of gold and the second largest producer of silver in the world. The Chinese government does not allow the export of gold and silver from China. What is mined in China stays in China. That production is not available for investors outside of China to buy.

Also, the central bank of China has been buying a great deal of gold the last couple of years. Why do I mention this in a chapter titled "The Better Case for Silver?" I do so to reiterate the point that there will not be enough gold to go around when the economic tsunami hits—and there is much, much less silver than there is gold.

Given the facts presented thus far in this chapter, you may wonder why the price of silver is so low compared to gold. The reason is price manipulation.

Price manipulation of silver, like gold, occurs in the futures markets. About thirty years ago a large U.S. bank bought, and has maintained, huge short positions in silver.

All price manipulation comes to an end eventually. But for as long as price manipulation continues in silver, a great buying opportunity exists. It is an opportunity to buy personal "asset protection insurance" against the coming inflation at a huge discount.

In summary, silver is required in ever-increasing quantities by industry. And mining production has flattened out. When only a small percentage of the $600 + trillion in world-wide assets (the value of all stocks, bonds, real estate, etc.) moves into physical silver for asset protection, there will be a critical shortage of physical silver. Industries will pay whatever it must to acquire the physical silver it needs to produce its products. The price of silver will rise dramatically. Industry will very likely begin hoarding physical silver, and perhaps big industry will try to buy silver mines of its own.

# 6     Classes of Silver Assets

In this chapter I will describe each primary class of silver asset. They are listed least desirable first.

Silver Futures Contracts

To speculate in silver futures, one must open a commodities trading account. Commodities traders have tremendous leverage, as much as 100:1. That is, they need only put up as little as $1 to control $100 worth of silver for a period of time.

Decades of data indicate that one has much better odds of success gambling in Las Vegas than playing the futures market. Trading silver futures is not a way to use silver to protect your assets. Technically, a silver futures contract is an asset. But no more so than that blackjack hand that you just bought (by placing a bet).

<u>I strongly recommend that you stay away from all futures trading, not just silver.</u>

Collectible Silver Coins

In difficult economic times, all manner of collectibles lose value. Buying collectible silver coins or other collectible silver articles is not asset protection in inflationary times. If the item has silver content, the value will always be at least the melt value of the silver, but the value of collectables will not increase as fast as the price of silver will.

When the economy is not in recession or depression, collectible coins can sell for a very large premium over the value of the silver content. As economic conditions worsen, many coin collectors will no longer be able to afford to collect. Demand for collectibles will decrease, and prices, relative to inflation, will also decrease. When demand decreases relative to supply, so do prices.

Silver Mining Stocks

As a class, silver mining stocks will do well over the long term. But picking the right silver mining stock/s is very difficult. If you have money in a self-directed IRA and want to invest a portion of it in silver, there are better ways to make a long-term investment in silver than silver mines ....

Electronic Traded Funds (ETFs)

ETFs are like a mutual fund but are bought and sold like a stock. An ETF usually holds several stocks in a single class or sector like mutual fund does. But unlike a mutual fund that can only be bought or sold after the market closes, ETFs are bought and sold during regular market hours.

There are silver ETFs that own only physical silver. When one buys shares of the ETF, one owns a share of the silver that the ETF owns.

Silver ETFs, like the price of silver, are very volatile.

There are also ETFs that own silver mining stocks. Naturally, they own those that the analysts believe will do best. If you decide you want to own silver mining stocks at some time, consider these ETFs instead of individual stocks.

Silver mining ETFs, like silver mining stocks, tend to be even more volatile than silver.

<u>I am not recommending the purchase of these or any other ETFs.</u> This book is not about investing, but about acquiring economic disaster insurance in the form of physical silver.

Physical Silver

Physical silver can be obtained in several forms.
　　　　NOTE: silver (and gold) is measured and priced in troy ounces
　　　　1 Troy ounce = 31.1 grams
　　　　　　Whereas;
　　　　1 standard ounce = 28.4 grams
　　　　(may also be referred to as an imperial ounce)

If you do the math, you will note that there are only 14.1 troy ounces in a pound instead of the 16 standard ounces you learned about in school in the U.S. or Great Britain.

The most common forms of physical silver available to Americans are listed below.

Bars – common sizes are 1 (troy) ounce, 5 ounce, ten ounce, 100 ounce, and 1,000 ounce.

Small bars are struck with many different designs by the different private mints that produce and sell them. Stay away from so-called collector designs and limited editions. What you want for economic disaster insurance is the most silver for the least cost per troy ounce.

Silver bars are usually .999% pure silver, which is as close to 100% pure as is practical.

All bars I have seen are rectangular, however …

Rounds – rounds are simply small round bars. They too, are struck in many designs. I have not seen a round greater than 10 ounces.

The rounds that I have seen are also .999 pure.

Despite the round shape, they are not coins or currency. They are just lumps of silver formed into a flat round shape with designs on the flat sides.

Bars and rounds are no longer my favorite form of physical silver, but if I can get them cheap, I do.

Pre-1965 U.S. coins – These are coins struck by the U.S. mint in years 1964 and earlier. We are speaking of the dime, quarter, half dollar, and dollar coins—not the nickel.

All of the above-mentioned coins are 90% silver. Below is a table showing the silver content of each coin when minted and the assumed silver content after it has been circulated.

| Coin | Mint content | circulated content |
|---|---|---|
| Dime | .0725 oz | .0715 oz |
| Quarter | .1813 oz | .1718 oz |
| ½ dollar | .3625 oz | .3575 oz |
| **$1 face** | **.7250 oz** | **.7150 oz** |

(*any combination of dimes, quarters, and half dollars that equals $1 face value*)

"$1 face" is printed in **bold** because that is the way these coins are sold in bags as silver bullion. A $1 face value in any combination of dimes, quarters, and half dollars had a silver content of 0.725 troy ounces at time of mint. Coins with average circulation contain only 0.715 ounces of silver due to wear.

That assumed wear is .010 ounces per $1 face. With silver at $50 per ounce, .010 ounces equals fifty cents, or 36 cents per one dollar face value of pre-1965 coins.

I have seen some sellers claim that circulated coins contain .720 ounces of silver. Maybe their coins have been circulated less, but I doubt it. The commonly accepted content of circulated coins is .715 troy ounces per $1 face value.

Buy circulated coins only. Non-circulated or graded coins are similar to "collector coins" and will cost much more per ounce of silver than circulated coins.

There are some "war nickels" that have some silver content. I do not recommend these as a source of silver bullion. I suspect the premium is high because they are rare. They are not silver bullion coins.

Some people call these circulated coins junk silver. The saying "One man's junk is another man's treasure" applies. I'll take all of this junk I can get.

The pre-1964 'silver dollar' is also 90% silver, as are the dime, quarter, and half dollar, but it contains more silver than $1 face of dimes, quarters, or half dollars.

| Coin | Mint content | circulated content |
|---|---|---|
| Dollar | .7735 oz | .7725 oz |

Why does the 90% dollar coin contain more silver that $1 face of the other 90% silver coins? Out of curiosity I researched it; it's complicated. I will not take time and space to explain the why.

Many silver dollars seem to be at least semi-collectable, as indicated by the price, which indicates a considerable premium over the silver content. Even worn, common silver dollars carry a high premium.

I do not recommend buying silver dollars. As with collectibles, I do not think the premiums will increase as fast as the price of silver. In my opinion, the premium, as a percentage of total value, will drop significantly on most silver dollars when the price of silver hits the stratosphere.

I like silver dollars, and do own a few obtained in lot purchases on eBay. For example; an $11.25 face value lot of pre-1965, 90% silver coins contained two or three silver dollars, and I won the auction.

40% Silver Half Dollars – Kennedy half dollars with mint years 1965, 1966, 1967, 1968, and 1969 contain 40% silver. They contain 0.295 ounces of silver per $1 face, or 0.1475 ounces each.

NOTE 1: The 1964 Kennedy half dollar contains 90% silver. The 1964 Kennedy half is the only Kennedy half that contains 90% silver.

NOTE 2: Kennedy halves minted in 1970 and beyond contain no silver. Do not buy them.

If you have seen any Kennedy half dollars minted 1969 or earlier, you may have noticed that they have very little wear. They were hoarded because of their popularity, and also for their silver content in the mid to late 1970s as the price of silver began to rise.

Silver Eagles – Silver Eagles are modern coins minted by the U.S. treasury. They are .999 pure, as are the bars and rounds minted by private mints. They qualify as U.S. currency. They are very popular among silver buyers in the U.S.

That they are pure silver shows that Silver Eagles are not intended to be used as currency because they will wear very fast. The popularity of Silver Eagles results in a relatively high premium over the melt value (silver content multiplied by the spot price of silver).

Most Silver Eagles are one (troy) ounce coins.  But recently I noticed that fractional silver eagles are being minted.  I suggest buying only one ounce coins because the premium on the smaller coins is even higher than on the one ounce coin.

This week at bulliondirect.com, my favorite internet dealer, one-ounce silver eagles sold at a 13.34% premium; 90% U.S. silver coins sold at an 11.22% premium; and 40% Kennedy halves sold at a 2.54% premium.

I have seen defective silver eagles from time-to-time.  The premium is a little lower.  For the purpose of protection against high inflation, defective silver eagles will work just as well as non-defective silver eagles.

You can't go wrong buying silver eagles.  The premium may hold in the future; at least in the U.S.  If you like silver eagles, paying a few percent more in premium will make little difference when the price of silver has shot skyward.  My personal preference is to buy the U.S. coins with the least premium over the spot price of silver.

CAUTION:  I notice that graded silver eagles are now being sold.  The highest grade I know of for a coin is MS70.  Though I know little about collector coins, I believe a MS70 coin is a perfect coin with zero wear.  A coin graded MS67 has some imperfections, and/or some slight wear.  A coin graded MS62 is little better than an average condition circulated coin (I think).

Do Not Buy Graded Silver Eagles.

At this time, an MS70 goes for about a 200% premium over melt value; an MS67 for about 100%. These are collector coins. If you are reading this book, you are not a coin collector, you are trying to survive the inflation-driven economic tsunami that is on the way.

# 7     A Simple Plan

*"Ants are creatures of little strength, yet they store up their food in the summer;"*
-Proverbs 30: 25


The simple plan is; **buy small amounts of physical silver regularly**; simple.

The American of modest means is struggling to stay even in this never-ending economic recession that began in 2008, and most are losing ground. After inflation, median income in the U.S. has dropped 7% since 2001—and inflation has been low.

Even those who have a well-funded 401k do not have the investment options available to protect those assets from the economic tsunami that is coming. The typical investment choices in a 401k are; stock funds, bonds, and money market funds, and they will all fare poorly when high inflation hits.

Real estate will lose value when interest rates rise. And interest rates will rise when inflation increases. It will be many years before real estate values bottom out and inflation finally takes the nominal dollar value of real estate back up. But in after-inflation dollars, the value will not be as much as it is at these historic low-interest times we are experiencing in early 2014.

In 1980, when silver hit $49 and change, for the value of 500 ounces of silver one could buy a median priced house in the U.S. Some predict that the time will come will again. I believe it. Today 500 ounces of silver is only worth about $11,000.

Take a few dollars and buy silver every pay day. How much? As much as you can. Don't stop buying until inflation takes your cost of living and the cost of silver up so much that the choice is food and shelter or silver.

If you cannot afford to buy any silver, cut costs somewhere, somehow, and use the money to buy silver. Sacrifice now to help secure the rest of your life. If you do not, you will be dependent on the government—and the government is already beyond broke.

If you think letting the U.S. government take care of you sounds good, visit an "Indian Reservation" and see how its working for Native American tribes.

# 8     What to buy

When I started buying silver I bought one ounce bars. The bars stack nicely, making them easy and space-efficient to store, and are generally available at a lower premium over melt value than other forms of physical silver.

The premium is the additional cost above the melt value. That is, if the spot price of silver is $40 per ounce, and the price of one ounce bars is $41 each, the premium is 2.5% ($41 - $40 = $1, and $1 divided by $40 = .025, which is 2.5%). Other forms of physical silver usually carry a higher premium over the melt value.

As I learned more about the disaster awaiting the U.S. dollar, my preference became pre-1965 U.S. 90% silver coins. I like them because the silver content is guaranteed by the U.S. mint. And the whole world trusts the U.S. mint—at least it did in the last century when these coins were struck.

It is not at all practical to counterfeit silver bars, especially the small ones. But when the price of silver hits the stratosphere and people become desperate, some may try. That may make selling bars, when the time comes for you to do so, a little more troublesome. Don't get me wrong, if I can buy silver bars at a bargain, I will. But my preference is U.S. coins, even though the premium is higher

At $40 an ounce, the melt value (value of the silver) of a 90% silver dime is $2.86. At $200 per ounce for silver, the melt value of a dime is $14.30.

In 2013 the premium on pre-1965 U.S. coins increased from about 5% to as high as 20%. The premium on bars increased too, but not by as much. I still prefer coins. I believe the premium will hold up going forward because of the utility of these coins. Everybody in North America recognizes and accepts the silver content of these coins.

To have 500 ounces of silver in the form of 90% circulated silver U.S. coins, one will need to accumulate $700 face value.

I particularly like the 1964 Kennedy halves. I like the size, the 'heft' of them. I also like the slightly greater silver content than the typical circulated pre-1965 coins. Because 1964 was the last year U.S. coins were minted with 90% silver, and because of the great popularity of the Kennedy halves, these coins did not get circulated nearly as much as those coins minted in the early sixties. And of course, coins minted in the forties and fifties got much greater circulation, and therefore, wear.

Less circulation means less wear. Consequently, when I buy circulated 90% Kennedy halves, I assume .720 ounces of silver instead of .715 ounces, which means I will pay a little more. The difference is only .005 ounces per dollar face value, or .0025 ounces per coin.

At $40 per ounce for silver, that .0025 ounces per coin is worth 10 cents. At $200 per ounce for silver, there is 50 cents more silver per 1964 Kennedy half dollar.

I believe silver will be worth so much in the years ahead, that when industry buys them in bulk to be melted down, these circulated coins will be bought by weight, not on the assumption of .715 ounces per dollar face value. Very old coins with a great deal of wear may contain only .710 per $1 face value. I think Kennedy halves contain .720 per $1 face value.

In 2012, when I was buying only 90% silver coins, and particularly 1964 Kennedy halves, I accidentally bought a couple of 40% Kennedy halves. I was also accidentally sent a couple of 40% Kennedy halves in a batch of 90% Kennedy halves that I bought (Upon contacting the seller I was promptly refunded the difference in value).

In 2012, I had such disdain for coins with only 40% silver content that I sold those that I acquired accidentally on eBay at my cost, or maybe a little less. Kennedy halves with only 40% silver content take as much space to store as those with 90% silver.

However, in 2013 when the premium on 90% silver U.S. coins increased to 20%, I found I could still buy 40% Kennedy halves at a 5% premium; about the same as .999 pure silver bars at the time.

A 40% Kennedy half dollar (mint dates of 1965, 1966, 1967, 1968, and 1969) contains .1475 ounces of silver. At $40 per ounce the melt value is $5.90. At $200 per ounce, it is $29.50 per coin. Acquiring 500 ounces of silver in the form of 40% Kennedy halves will require $1,700 face value, or 3,400 Kennedy half coins.

I decided that paying a much lower premium was worth the additional storage space.

*40% silver Kennedy half dollars – my current favorite*

Another reason that I like pre-1965 coins and 40% half dollars is that they are legal tender in the U.S.

Some people are concerned that gold will once again become illegal for Americans to own. I have my doubts about that happening. But if gold ownership does become illegal, could silver also become illegal to own? If it comes to that, I should think it would be much more difficult for the U.S. to make its own coinage illegal to own than other forms of silver.

In summary, I prefer U.S. minted coins with 90% silver content or 40% silver content, but recommend buying common forms of physical silver at the best premium you can find.

# 9    Where to Buy

Disclaimer: I am not associated in any way, other than as a satisfied customer, with any sources mentioned below. I receive no compensation or recognition of any type from any of these silver bullion suppliers.

Private Mints

A private mint, as opposed to the U.S. mint, is a company that buys precious metals in bulk and produces bars, rounds, commemorative medals, and other items. Many private mints also deal in U.S. 90% silver coins. There are several reputable mints in the U.S., and I have bought from a couple of them before finding other sources more suited to my needs and strategy.

Buying from a mint posed two problems for my plan of buying small quantities often. First, buying small quantities meant higher premiums. At that time, the price of silver was rising rapidly. If I saved to buy a larger quantity at a lower premium, I paid a higher price for silver.

Second, I had to wait weeks after payment to receive my silver bars.

I understand waiting weeks to receive minted bars, which is what I bought when I began my plan. The private mint buys bulk silver and schedules production of the particular design I ordered. However, when I started buying coins, I found that I also had to wait weeks to receive them. The private mint doesn't mint pre-1965 U.S. coins. The U.S. Treasury minted those coins decades ago. I didn't like the private mint working off of my money for six to eight weeks.

No doubt there are some mints that ship pre-1965 coins quickly. Just be aware of, and satisfied with, the policy before you buy from a private mint. The minimum purchase may be too high to accommodate a strategy of buying a small quantity often.

Local Dealers

In California, if the total sale is under $1,500, sales tax must be charged. In California, sales tax is 8% to 9%, depending on locale. I am not willing to pay a high sales tax on top of the premium. On the other hand, there is no shipping and handling as may be the case with other sources.

Your state of residence may be different. In Maryland the magic number that allows you to avoid sales tax is $1,000. Check it out before you buy. Just call a local coin dealer and ask.

Even if sales tax is not an issue in your state, compare the premium to other sources that are practical to you. And don't let them 'sell you' on the idea of buying "collectible" coins or mint condition coins! And don't buy anything that is graded (MSxx).

## eBay

I have purchased a great deal of the silver I have accumulated so far in small quantities from eBay auctions. I have never seen a good "buy it now" price for gold or silver on eBay. I have never been cheated. On one occasion two 40% silver Kennedy half dollar coins got mixed with the 90% Kennedy half dollars that I bought. The seller apologized and promptly refunded the difference in value upon my notification.

On another occasion I didn't read the posting carefully enough and bought two 40% Kennedy halves in a lot along with several 1964 Kennedy halves.

I buy from sellers who have very high positive feedback; 98% to 100%. I have taken a chance on new sellers on small purchases a few times, and have never been disappointed.

I no longer buy from eBay sellers in California, my state of residence, because I do not want to deal with the possibility of being charged sales tax. Many bullion and bullion coin sellers on eBay also have a brick-and-mortar store. If that store is in California, they must charge sales tax to California residents on purchases of less than $1,500. Be sure you know the facts before bidding on silver sold by sellers in your state of residence.

When I first started buying on eBay I would ask California sellers, through eBay's "ask seller a question," if they would charge me sales tax if my bid won. However, that was a hassle I decided I did not need since there were plenty of out-of state coins up for auction.

Buyer Beware – there are a number of things to be aware of when buying silver on eBay. More of them are especially relevant to buying 90% or 40% silver coins than silver bars or rounds. But once aware, it takes just a few seconds of careful reading to ensure you know what is being auctioned.

1. Shipping cost. Some shipping costs are very high relative to the value of the item. I calculate the cost as a percentage of the total cost, or as the cost per ounce of silver or cost per piece of Kennedy half. It does me little good to win the silver at a 10% premium over the spot price of silver and then pay 20% of the purchase price for shipping. I might as well have gone down to my local coin dealer, even if I do have to pay 8.75% sales tax.

I like bidding on items that have "free" shipping or have very low shipping costs. When I have bid on items with a high shipping cost, there is always at least one buyer bidding against me that doesn't pay attention to shipping costs. I no longer waste my time bidding on silver that has a high shipping cost. I never win because I place a bid that keeps my total cost in line with competitive prices for the same item from my other sources.

2. Sales Tax. Will you be charged and if so, at what percent?

3. Ounces of silver. <u>This is a big one</u>, especially on 90% silver coins. There are many auctions that advertize something like, "4 ozs. Pre-1965 Silver Coins."

First, four ounces of silver coins is not four ounces of silver. The coins are only 90% silver by weight. Four troy ounces of silver coins is only 3.6 troy ounces of silver.

Second, are the four ounces being sold troy ounces or standard ounces? If it is four standard ounces of 90% silver coins, and it usually is, then you are getting only about 3.28 troy ounces of silver. 3.28 ounces is 18% less than 4 ounces.

A few years ago I would calculate the troy ounces of silver content on these auctions and bid, but I never won. There are apparently many people who do not understand the above-mentioned facts. I no longer bid on coins listed in this manner.

Do not bid on 90% silver coins without knowing the face value of what is being sold. You may have the math skills to calculate the melt value of a lot of coins listed by total weight, but there will be at least one buyer bidding against you who does not, and they will think they are bidding on 18% more silver than is the case.

Another way to approach bidding is by face value of the coins being offered. A dollar face value of any combination pre-1965 dimes, quarters, or half dollar coins contains 0.715 troy ounces of silver. To determine the value of the silver content, multiply the face value by 0.715, and multiply the product by the spot price of silver.

Example: If face value is $3.75 and the spot price of silver is $35.55;

$3.75 face value x 0.715 x $35.55 spot price of silver = $95.32

That is the melt value of the silver in that particular lot of coins; $95.32

I do not win a high percentage of the lots of coins on which I enter bids. Therefore, I usually bid on multiple lots. If you plan on doing the same, you may want to calculate the melt value of one dollar face value and then multiply that value by the face amount of the particular lot.

Example: If the spot price of silver is $35.55;

$35.55 x 0.715 = $25.42 melt value per $1 face value

If a particular lot is $1.75 face value, multiply $25.42 x $1.75. The melt value of that particular lot is $44.48 (same as the example above).

If a lot contains three quarters and two dimes, which is $0.95 face value; $25.42 x $0.95 face value = $24.15.

By doing the math, you will note that $1.40 face value of pre-1965 silver coins contains one troy ounce of silver. This is another handy reference. You can divide the face value being auctioned by 1.4 to determine how much silver you will receive.

Example: If $2.00 face value is offered; 2.00 divided by 1.4 = 1.43 troy ounces of silver content. If the spot price of silver is $40 per ounce, then the melt value is 1.43 ounces x $40 = $57.14.

Naturally, you will have to bid more than $57.14 to win the action.

How much over melt value should you bid? Right now, with the price of silver in the low $20s, it really doesn't matter too much. Years from now, when the price of silver is over $200 an ounce, the fact that you paid a few percent more on premium now will be insignificant.

Basically, pay the average price that you observe wins many auctions. If total cost per ounce or dollar of face value is less at your local dealer, go to your local dealer. More important than a couple of percentage points of premium is that you buy regularly.

DO NOT buy "Unsearched Coins." Sellers go to the bank and get rolls of quarters or half dollars and sell them as "unsearched." You will not find enough (probably absolutely none) pre-1965 coins to break even on the minimum purchase price plus shipping. Twenty years ago this may have been a reasonable bet, but not today.

Before I bid on eBay, I check the cost at my favorite source and bid accordingly. For me at this time, my favorite source is sometimes a viable alternative because I can buy enough silver at one time to make the handling and shipping cost a relatively small percentage of total cost. My favorite source is Bullion Direct.

www.bulliondirect.com

At bulliondirect.com, one can buy as little as $10 face value of pre-1965 U.S. silver coins or 40% Kennedy halves. However, buyers must have the items shipped within three weeks of purchase. At this time there is a $9.95 handling fee plus actual shipping costs (insurance is included in the handling fee).

Before bidding on eBay, I check the spot price of silver and the cost of silver coins at bullionidrect.com.

Although the premium over spot is less than any other source I have found, this may not be the best source if you have only a few dollars to spend. The handling and shipping costs may add too much per ounce of silver.

Bullion Direct is located in Austin, Texas. There are two ways to buy. One is through its Nucleo

Exchange. Here members buy and sell from each other. It costs nothing to become a member. Both buyer and seller pay a 1% fee to Bullion Direct on each transaction. Sellers must have the item/s they are selling on-hand at Bullion Direct before placing it for sale. Payment for items bought is by personal check payable to Bullion Direct.

The other way to buy is from the Bullion Direct catalog. Their premiums are the lowest I have seen, and the minimum purchase quantity is lower than mints or other on-line dealers I have investigated. For example, you can buy a single one ounce silver bar for the same premium as a purchase of 100 one ounce bars. But again, the handling and shipping on a single bar is very high as a percentage of the purchase price of a single bar.

My investigation of on-line dealers is not exhaustive. I have bought "introductory" offers two times from other on-line dealers. Their regular prices were not better than Bullion Direct, so I have not bought from either of them again. There are many reputable on-line dealers. But the problems for "buyers of modest means" buying small quantity often are; the handling/shipping costs, and the potentially high premium on a small quantity.

Therefore, local coin dealers or eBay are probably the best sources for an American of modest means.

However, be sure you know what percent premium you are paying over the melt value. Many dealers have it posted. Many will have a website at which it is posted.

## 10      Safe Storage of Your Silver

Generally speaking, the options to safely store your silver are; in a safe, in a safety deposit box, and hide it.  Each of these options has variations, and two or more options can be used in combination.  As your holdings grow, you may use two or more options.  The discussion below is not exhaustive, but should get the thinking process started.


Home Safe

The safes that you see for sale at office supply and home improvement centers are mostly, if not all, fire safes.  Most have a one hour fire rating for paper.  They are easy to break into.

The older fire safes have a thick double wall with wet clay between the walls.  These safes are not heavy because the walls are made of heavy steel as one might assume, but because of the wet clay.  Holes can be drilled through the thin metal walls and wet clay with a household drill.  Doors can generally be broken into with a strong pry bar.  If not secured to the floor or wall, these safes can be carried away and broken into at the thief's leisure.

However, a sizable safe full of silver would be quite heavy.  A cubic foot of pure silver weighs about 655 pounds.

Placing the safe in a hard-to-get-at place will make it more difficult for a thief to break into.

A better solution is to hide the safe. Unless a thief knows there is a hidden safe full of treasures, they aren't likely to spend a lot of time looking. Since this book is written for the American of modest means, I assume you are not living in a mansion in a swanky gated community.

About fire -- The typical house fire burns between 1,400 and 1,500 degrees Fahrenheit. The melting point of silver is about 1,760 degrees Fahrenheit. If your house burns down, you will not be left with a big lump of charred silver that is too heavy to carry.


Safety Deposit Box

Banks in my area seem to only rent safety deposit boxes to those who have an account at the bank. My medium size box costs me $45 per year.


Hide It

I don't recommend hiding your silver under your mattress. It's hard enough to get a good night's sleep without bags or piles of silver bars adding to the problem.

Burying it in the yard is a possibility. When considering this option I decided I would collect scrap metal and bury pieces all around the yard, just in case somebody came around with a metal detector. I found better solutions before my safety deposit box filled up.

Another solution I considered was burying silver in the crawl space under my house. The only access to the crawl space under my house is very small. Since there is the single access, it would take a lot of belly crawling for a thief to search the whole area.

I also considered putting a safe or strong box in a corner of the crawl space and bricking it in so that only the recessed door to the strong box showed. There is no room for demolition in my crawl space. And why would petty thieves even look?

Why do I say "petty thieves?" I say it because high-end thieves wouldn't want to be seen just driving through my neighborhood. It would ruin their reputation. And again, I found better solutions.


Store with Someone You Trust

I know some trustworthy people who have a big safe and lots of guns. As my holdings outgrew my safety deposit box, I spread my holdings out by placing a portion of my silver with these trusted individuals. My silver is scattered among five locations in four different states.

Do not let people know that you are accumulating silver. If you have children, do not tell them that you are accumulating silver. This advice may seem silly now, but when the economy is coming apart at its seams and unemployment is 40%, many people will become desperate.

In summation; President Ronald Reagan famously asserted, "The nearest thing to eternal life we will ever see on this earth is a government program."

We can be sure that;

Overspending by the government will not stop.

Money creation will not cease.

The Federal budget will not be balanced.

The resulting inflation will destroy the assets of Americans as well as America's economy.

**Start now.**

www.ingramcontent.com/pod-product-compliance
Lightning Source LLC
Chambersburg PA
CBHW071803170526
45167CB00003B/1153